DELERE

This paperback edition first published in 2013 by Delere Press

Illustrations and layout copyright © Chan Yin Wan
Text copyright © Jeremy Fernando

First published in 2013 by Delere Press

Delere Press LLP
370G Alexandra Road #09-09
Singapore 159960
www.delerepress.com

Delere Press LLP Reg No. T11LL1061K

ISBN 978-981-07-4309-3

On invisibility;

or, towards a minor jiu-jitsu.

Text by Jeremy Fernando
Illustrations and layout by Yanyun Chen

DELERE PRESS

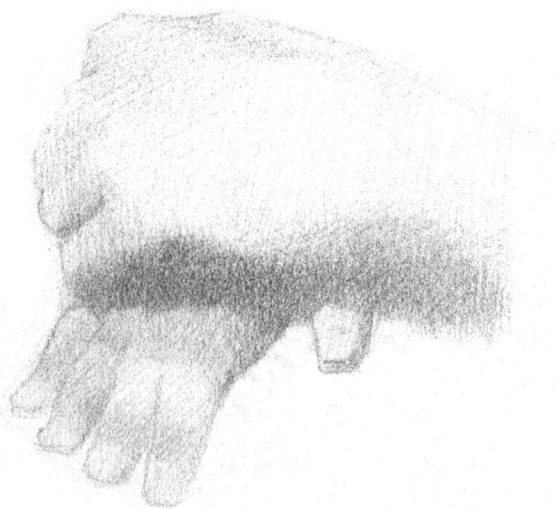

For Sharon 'Meow' Bonewicz
Who showed me years ago—through her work with the
Rocinha Project—the art in jiu-jitsu
And for that, I remain always grateful …

AZUL

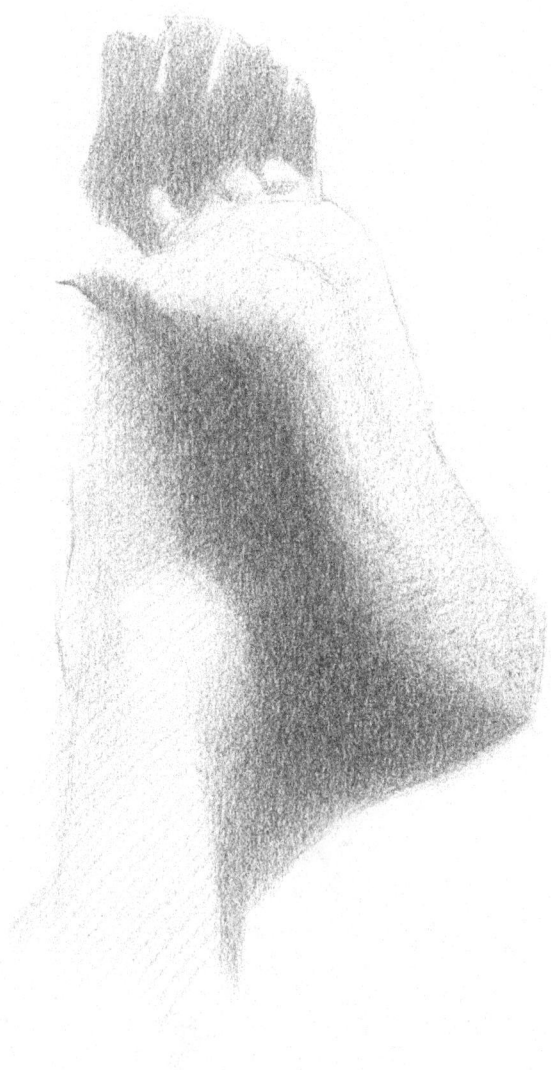

The great stars or seductresses never dazzle because of their talent or intelligence, but because of their absence.
(Jean Baudrillard: *Seduction*)

An absence that dazzles.

Which suggests dazzling comes not so much from the source—from an object at which one is looking—but from the one who is looking. Perhaps what truly dazzles the one who looks is the very act of looking itself. Even more than that, perhaps the one who is dazzled can only break the spell by looking elsewhere.

And what else is jiu-jitsu but a manner of ensnaring your adversary—of luring another into what you want them to do, where you want them to be, of making them look anywhere, pay attention to anything, but the place they should. We can hear this echoed in Rillion Gracie's strategy: "I specialised in leaving an opening for the guy to pass, as that is the moment he exerts force—and so he wears out and falls in a trap."[1] In focusing on, looking at, the alleged opening, one fails to see, one is blind to, the web that the other has set; to entrap. And in that way one practically forces oneself into the snare. One sets the trap—the rest is up to the one who ends up trapped.

Dazzle-painting. Camouflage.

One is trapped precisely because one is seduced by the possibility of the opening. Which is not to say that the possibility is empty, nothingness, null: after all, there is always a chance one might jump the fence, pass the guard. But more radically, it is the fact that it appears as nothing that makes it seductive. What is dazzling, what makes one look, is precisely this absence. Which makes one see more than what is there: the trap is precisely in letting one make meaning where there is none. This suggests that one picks the very manner in which one is trapped: the trap is a form; the content one writes oneself.

Armbars, chokes, footlocks—anything, everything, is possible.

In Robert Goodman's documentary *Choke*,[2] one of Rickson Gracie's students and training partners enthused that just because you knew what Rickson was going to do did not mean you could stop it. In fact, he could tell you exactly what he would attempt, start counting down, and he would still get you in it. Is this not precisely what one faces every time one encounters a good magician? Even if one knows what (s)he is about to do, one is not able to tell how (s)he is doing it. The feeling of helplessness is compounded if one actually takes the time to study the mechanics of the illusion—just because one knows what is going to happen to one does not always mean that one can do anything about it.

It would be erroneous to say that the error of Rickson's student was in paying too much attention to defending the technique that was called out. That would have been true if he was caught in a different submission. The fact that Rickson would submit you with precisely what he called out opens an infinitely more profound proposition: his student was dazzled in the absence of any surprise; he was dazzled precisely because there was nothing to dazzle him with.

Not only is the source of the dazzling invisible, so is the very reason for one being dazzled. All one can say is: one was seduced.

It is this unknowable aspect of the art that Rickson
Gracie encapsulates in the elegant name he has given
his approach: "invisible jiu-jitsu." An approach which
acknowledges that part of the art always lies outside the
person; an intuitive aspect that can only be glimpsed
momentarily through years and years of rolling, feeling,
touching. And it is for this reason that jiu-jitsu is *arte
suave*—the gentle art. Whilst many have focused on its
efficiency, on gentleness, on leverage, it is Rickson that
reminds us that jiu-jitsu is first and foremost an art—in
the precise sense of a craft at its highest level, where it
consumes the practitioner, often in ways which are exterior
to one's cognitive ability.

And it is this insight—born of experience—that allows Rickson to claim, somewhat controversially, that jiu-jitsu is all one needs in a fight. Wanderlei Silva, for instance, has responded that despite being a fan of Rickson, he also thinks that the latter is living in a fantasy world: the modern day sport of mixed martial arts has evolved too much for anyone proficient in just one style, no matter what, to win.

This is where Wanderlei has missed the point.

For, when Rickson is speaking of a fight he is hardly speaking of a sport. More importantly, Rickson's claim is indicative of the fact that when he speaks of jiu-jitsu as a martial art, his focus is on art. Naturally, fighting—the martial—is fundamental. As Relson Gracie famously quipped, "we aren't teaching dancing here." The ability to fight, to defend oneself, is the craft that the artisans of jiu-jitsu seek to develop. However, at its highest level—at the point when craft becomes art—it transcends technique, *tekhnē*, in the precise sense that it is always also potentially universal.

Here, it might be helpful to turn to an unusual source
when it comes to fighting: the philosopher Immanuel
Kant. When Wanderlei claims that one needs a variety of
skills—stand-up, clinch, grappling, conditioning, etc.—
to do well in MMA, he is appealing to what Kant calls a
private use of reason. This is a reason that is contingent
on presuppositions, situations, and so forth. When
Rickson claims that jiu-jitsu is all one needs in a fight, he is
appealing to a *universality*, a truth; a reason that by-passes
the mediation of a particular. As Slavoj Žižek explains:
"This is what Kant, in the famous passage of his 'What is
Enlightenment?' means by *public* as opposed to *private*.
Private is not one's individual as opposed to communal
ties, but the very communal-institutional order of one's
particular identification; while *public* is the transnational
universality of the exercise of one's reason."[3]

This is not to say that Wanderlei is wrong: far from it. However, he is speaking of fighting from a particular point of view: that of a *muay thai* fighter who has learned how to grapple and is training to deal with a particular fighter who has a certain set of skills. Rickson is speaking of fighting and jiu-jitsu interchangeably: jiu-jitsu is fighting; fighting is jiu-jitsu. The gentle art is the definition of fighting. In this sense, when Rickson's jiu-jitsu is described as *out of this world*, those who are praising him are actually saying exactly the same thing as Wanderlei: the *fantasy* is precisely the ability to imagine fighting beyond the realm of two (or more) persons facing each other—it is a thinking of fighting that moves from the realm of physical engagement to one that is literally out of this world.

Perhaps here, it might be helpful to return for a moment to our detour and allow Kant's meditation on the French Revolution to resound with us. In the 'Conflict of Faculties' (1795), he enthuses: "the recent Revolution of a people which is rich in spirit, may well either fail or succeed, accumulate misery and atrocity, but nevertheless arouses in the heart of all spectators (who are not themselves caught up in it) a taking of sides according to desires which borders on enthusiasm and which, since its very expression was not without danger, can only have been caused by a moral disposition within the human race."[4] In other words, the power of the French Revolution lies in opening the imagination(s) of people to other possibilities—to a world without absolute monarchy. Whether the actual event succeeded or not is perhaps irrelevant. Similarly, it is only after the failed revolution of the slave-warrior Spartacus that the possibility of a *citizen-slave* could even be conceived.[5] In the same vein, whether a fight is won or loss is perhaps irrelevant: each time one conceives of jiu-jitsu as fighting (and fighting as jiu-jitsu), one's imagination is opened, just a little more.

This opening is only aroused, however, when one is "not … caught up in it." Hence, this is an opening to possibilities that might only be glimpsed at retrospectively, or even never at all. There is, after all, no guarantee that one can ever maintain enough of a distance to be open. For, at the point of the event—the fight—the possibilities remain invisible.[6]

This invisibility, unknowability—exterior to one's cognition—that echoes throughout the art is exemplified by the absolute trust in a teacher to grade students. In many cases, there is no reason to hand out a belt except for the fact that the teacher *feels that the student is ready.* Hence, the grading system is intuitive. Since the belt carries the name of the teacher, this suggests that by awarding it, the teacher is also putting her reputation on the line. It is no coincidence that the black belt has been equated with earning a PhD: both are stages where the student has nominally achieved her *viva voce,* voice of life. When one is awarded a black belt, the teacher is also saying *now you are ready to express jiu-jitsu in your own way, in your own voice.* This sentiment is captured beautifully in Royce Gracie's famous quip: "the belt only covers two inches of your ass; the rest you have to cover yourself."

However, with its escalating popularity, jiu-jitsu is starting to face its own monsters. The huge demand for instruction has led to many fraudulent individuals claiming to be 'BJJ black belts'. There are two main approaches to this very real problem and their varying natures allow us to catch a glimpse of the divergent philosophies within jiu-jitsu:

1.

The late Helio Gracie famously wore a blue belt whenever he was in Brazil "out of protest against the proliferation of Brazilian Jiu-Jitsu 'experts' and self proclaimed 'Gracie' stylists who are polluting the once crystal clear spring of knowledge that [I] perfected."[7] He continues, "the only method of Jiu-Jitsu teaching that I endorse is the one practiced by my sons ... [and] the only certified teachers that I endorse are those who have earned their teacher certification from me or my son Rorion."[8]

2.

On the surface, Carlos Gracie Jr. has a similar approach to the problem. By helming the *Confederação Brasileira de Jiu-jitsu* (CBJJ) which eventually led to the International Brazilian Jiu-Jitsu Federation (IBJJF), there has been an attempt to standardise jiu-jitsu. Organising jiu-jitsu under an overarching structure has allowed practitioners all over the world to have a much better idea of who is qualified to teach—thus, letting them choose their teachers with a more learned approach. Here, one can even hear an echo of his uncle Helio, and his declaration that the popularity of jiu-jitsu should not "provide an opportunity for unqualified people to fool the public by misrepresenting their ability as teachers."[9]

However, the similarities disappear when you take into consideration the notion of time; in particular, time spent between belts. By virtue of the logic of standardisation, the IBJJF has to issue a minimum time to be spent between promotions: the implication is that there is a correlation between one's belt level and the time one has spent in jiu-jitsu. By Helio Gracie's logic though, a belt—like the kind of instruction that you receive from himself and his sons—is an indication of level, of ability. And this is precisely where they differ: in Carlinhos one finds a trust in a system; in Helio, trust lies in the individual.

In itself, there is no problem with their respective
approaches. What they offer us though, is a glimpse
at differing implications for thought, exploration, and
questions. If there is an over-arching structure, thought
is always already within boundaries, within borders—by
extension, there is a notion (whether actualised or not)
of what jiu-jitsu is, and what it is not. When the thinking
is located in, and through, an individual, this suggests
that it is a singular approach towards jiu-jitsu, one that
is discovered through a person, and might in fact only
be known by that person. Thus, the role of the teacher
is to guide, whilst allowing one to seek one's own path,
method. And here, one should never forget that question,
and quest, have the same root, *questa* (search, inquiry);
that method comes *meta hodos* (over a path). As Saulo
Ribeiro once said, "I can teach someone everything I know
about jiu-jitsu in three months. But what I can't teach
is the timing, that comes from experience."[10] And the
"experience" is, of course, related to time, but a personal
time, a time that is singular to each person.

In *Choke*, there is a moment when Rickson Gracie utters a strange phrase, at least in the English language: "flow with the go." At that moment his insight as an artist of the lever shines through: it is one's singular response to the movement—of yourself, of the other—that is the very apex of jiu-jitsu. And this is precisely why timing is always emphasised: when you "flow with the go," you are doing nothing but finding (your own) time.

But since speaking directly of art might be beyond us— after all, Plato teaches us that the movement of craft to art requires the whisper of the *daemon*; thus, outside our cognition, knowledge, control—we can only speak of craft, *praxis*. The *praxis* of jiu-jitsu is leverage: the artisan is one who finds leverage in a way that no one else does; (s)he is the one that can feel precisely when, and at what point, to insert that lever. It is only felt as it happens, as it is happening: situationally, singularly. And at this moment, the artisan of the lever reifies time. This is *finding time* in the very precise sense of *discovering the moment itself*—a moment that doesn't exist before that; a moment that is written not by, but through, the artisan. And at that very moment, the craft becomes art.

For, at the highest level, not only is jiu-jitsu invisible to the eye, it remains invisible to one; it expresses itself through one.

And, it is a poetic approach to jiu-jitsu that opens the register that the gentle art is also *arte bela*, the beautiful art; for, what is art if it is not enigmatic.

ROXA

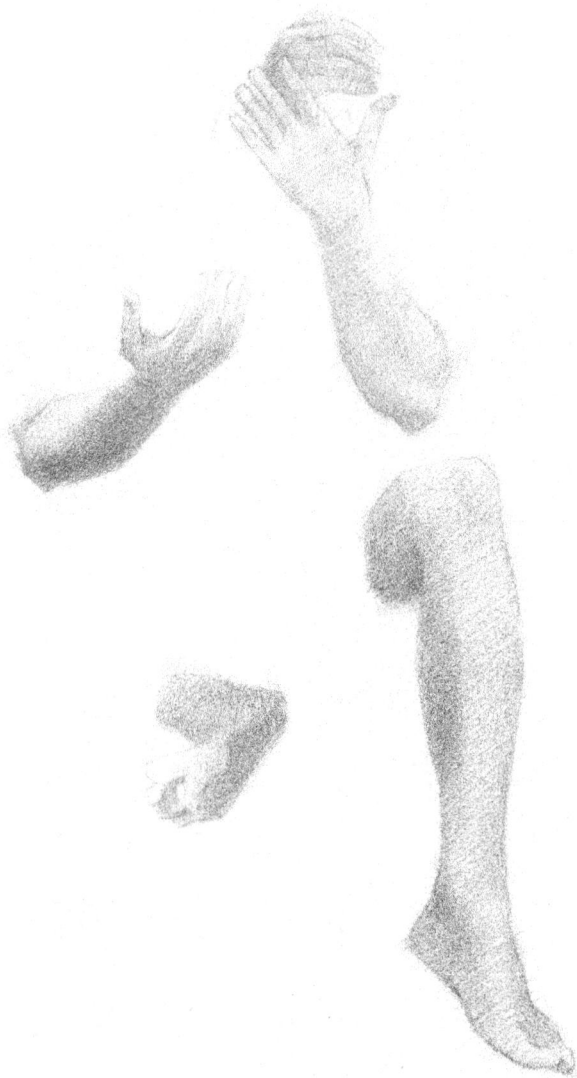

Since the language is arid, make it vibrate with a new intensity. Oppose a purely intensive usage of language to all symbolic or even significant or simply signifying usages of it.
(Gilles Deleuze & Félix Guattari: *Kafka: Toward a Minor Literature*)

We must never forget that both Jigaro Kano and the Gracie Brothers were not traditionalists. Far from it. They were heretics.

In this sense, the very *spirit* of both judo and jiu-jitsu is that of questioning.

Questioning arts—arts of questioning.

And as art only occurs through its *praxis*, this suggests that
art is neither a metaphysical nor an ontological notion:
it is not governed, controlled, by an over-arching idea. It
is not stagnant. This also suggests that art is situational:
each expression of an art is singular; and can, at best, only
be known at the moment of expression. We are blind
to it until it happens; perhaps even after its occurrence.
Moreover, there is no guarantee of repetition; for, even if
repeated, it might well be a repetition that is not the same.
Perhaps then, there is no more appropriate term for art
than *invisible*.

Which suggests that all we do—all we can do—is stumble around in the dark. For, even as we are questioning, even as there is a path to this quest, it is one that is immanent. This means that even if one is given—to borrow Lloyd Irvin's term—a "grappling blueprint," even if Saulo Ribeiro teaches you everything he knows, they are, at best, signposts. And that even as one's teacher guides, (s)he can only attempt to help one develop the ability to discover one's path: in terms of being on the quest, one is very much on one's own. Hence, whenever a teacher awards a belt, (s)he is staking her name on her student, on one. Since the timing is immanent, and more than that, can only be known at the moment of its application, there is no way to know for sure if the student is at that level (which is a universal notion) or not. Thus, the awarding of a belt, which is an endorsement of a general level—one which the teacher, and recipient of the belt, cannot be aware of until it happens—always already occurs in blindness.

This is why there is so much emphasis on whom one gets one's belt from. By awarding it, the teacher is demonstrating blind faith in that student. And this is why it is so apt that jiu-jitsu maintains the term *professor*. For, this is not just teaching in the sense of imparting a system of knowledge, but a declaration in the strictest sense of a profession of faith—both in the art, and also in the person receiving the lesson. And within every belt ceremony— each time a professor awards her student a belt—lies a moment in which (s)he declares, *this is my student.*

Thus, each time a professor ties a new belt around her student's waist, we hear echoes of the apex of jiu-jitsu: a moment when it transcends craft—a moment of art— where it remains invisible to everyone, except perhaps to, quite possibly even to, the person(s) in that moment.

Which means: each time one reaches the level of art, one is not only moving beyond the craft, the system, one is re-writing the system, the craft: one is re-writing what jiu-jitsu itself is. One is making jiu-jitsu "vibrate with a new intensity"[11]—opposing it "to all symbolic or even significant or simply signifying usages of it."[12] This is beyond giving jiu-jitsu new meaning: this is a pure expression of jiu-jitsu that is beyond meaning. Naturally, after it happens, it can be restored to, rehabilitated back under, the order of things, to reason even; it can be retrospectively understood.

Sometimes even named.

The *de la Riva guard*.

Roleta's *weird jiu-jitsu*.

But it is not as if Ricardo de la Riva nor Roberto 'Roleta' Magalhaes were doing a jiu-jitsu that was different from any other. From the very beginning everyone knew that both of them were attempting to sweep—it is no coincidence that de la Riva's approach was first termed the *wobbly guard*—and to destabilise. However, there is also no doubt that today's guard strategies could not have come about without their interventions. And here, we can once again hear echoes of Deleuze and Guattari and, in particular, their teaching that "a minor literature doesn't come from a minor language; it is rather that which a minority constructs within a major language."[13] What de la Riva and Roleta did was not just to invent new ways of sweeping, they destabilised the very notion of sweeping itself; and in doing so, opened a new world, with new possibilities, within sweeps.

Which brings us back to where we started. And to the fact that neither the Gracie Brothers nor Jigaro Kano were attempting to create entirely new styles: they were mixing, matching, remixing. It is only due to the intensities of their mixes—their questions—that made the systems they were enquiring—and eventually, the systems of their enquiry—tremble.

DJ Kano (feat jiu-jitsu): judo

DJ Carlos Gracie (feat Mitsuyo Maeda): jiu-jitsu[14]

DJ Helio (feat Carlos Gracie): jiu-jitsu.

Who ever said that the same name had to be the same?

For, one should never forget that as the DJ spins,
(s)he touches, feels—there is tactility to the tunes that are
emanating through the turntable. (S)he not only listens for
the beat, (s)he not only feels for the groove—both of the
record, and the track—(s)he grooves to the very beat:
(s)he and the beat are indistinguishable. And, at her ze-
nith, the line between her and the music becomes less and
less visible.

Scratch.[15]

But all of this happens at the same time, in the same instance. Behind your back, as it were. Invisible to you.

And, all you feel is the beat.

MARROM

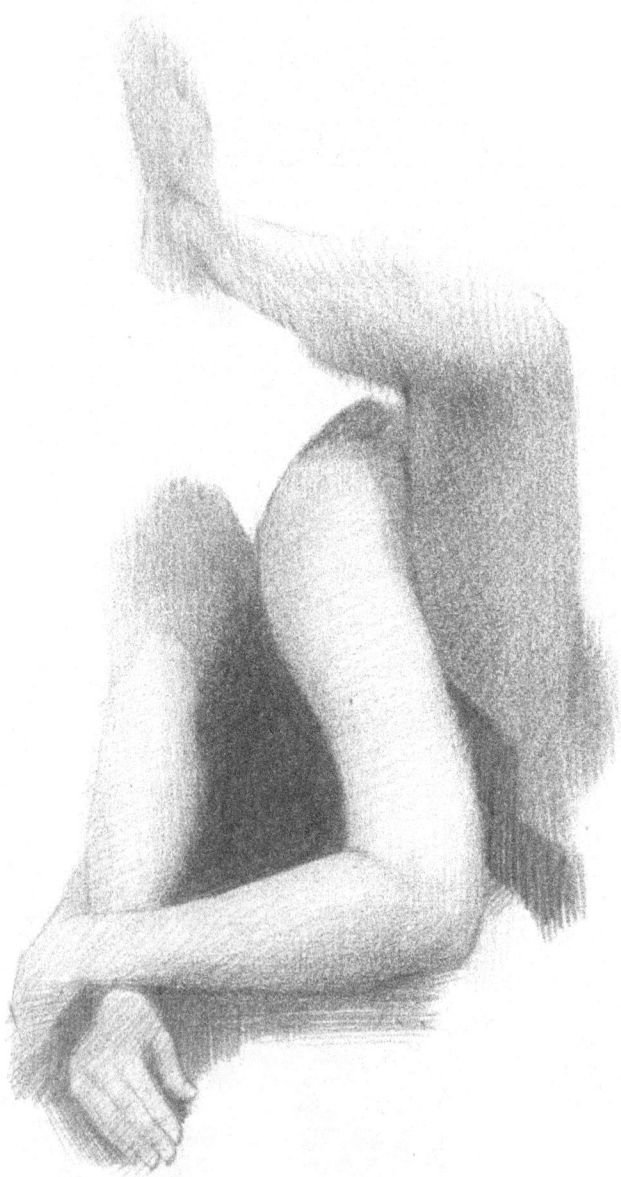

*The work ... stands under its own law of production
and is its own proof.*
(Jacques Rancière: *The Aesthetic Unconscious*)

If I am accused of attempting an aesthetic thinking of
jiu-jitsu, I plead guilty. And, more specifically, attempting
to think aesthetics in the sense that Jacques Rancière
proposes: "a mode of thought that develops with respect
to things of art and that is concerned to show them to be
things of thought."[16] It differs from logic in the precise
manner that it includes indistinct, unclear, knowledge—a
knowability that remains veiled. Rancière continues: "art
[is the] territory of a thought that is present outside itself
and identical with non-thought."[17] This non-thought
is hardly a lesser form of knowledge, "but properly *the
thought of that which does not think.*"[18] And what else is a
thinking of something that does not think other than an
attempt to think of something that is there (otherwise it
cannot be a thing) but which remains invisible to thought
itself. More crucially, this non-thought is a "thought
effectuated by works of art"[19]—a thought that is opened by
the thing. This is a thinking about fighting, about jiu-jitsu,
that comes from jiu-jitsu, from fighting, itself.

More importantly, since fighting is the thing and there is a "non-thought" that is identical with thinking, one can posit that this "non-thought" is quite possibly always already a part of thought itself. It is a part of thought that potentially remains invisible from thought; a part that thought is blind to. Or even: it is a part of thought that remains potentially invisible. So, even as we may be able to locate what cannot be thought, even if we can see what cannot be seen, this does not mean there is anything we can say about it. Thus, even as the work "is its own proof" we are never able to say, with any certainty, that a work is art.

Perhaps here, we can posit that the medium is precisely the site of this "non-thought"; and this is why art is a work of "unconditional creativity [which] is identified with an absolute passivity."[20] Thus, when we say that Rickson Gracie is a grappling genius, we should not forget "Kant's conception of genius [which] summarizes this duality. The genius is the active power of nature who sets his own creative power against any model or norm. The genius, we might say, becomes a norm for himself. But at the same time he is the one who does not know what he does and is incapable of accounting for his own activity."[21] This is precisely why Rickson emphasises technique over everything else: it is only when one pays attention to the details—to every movement—that one can forget the self and allow the art to express itself. As the Romans taught us, genius, inspiration, only happens to one—at the moment when the *genus* (who lives in the walls) chooses to comes to one. We have no control over when, where, or even if, it ever happens. Hence, one should take the separation of the person from the work all the way to the end; and posit that Rickson's jiu-jitsu has absolutely nothing to do with him as a person. That even though he is the medium, at the point when the *genus* whispers into his ear he "does not know what he does"; the point when he is a genius is the point at which Rickson Gracie is no longer Rickson Gracie.

He is a genius at the point where, the moment in which, he is invisible to himself.

PRETA

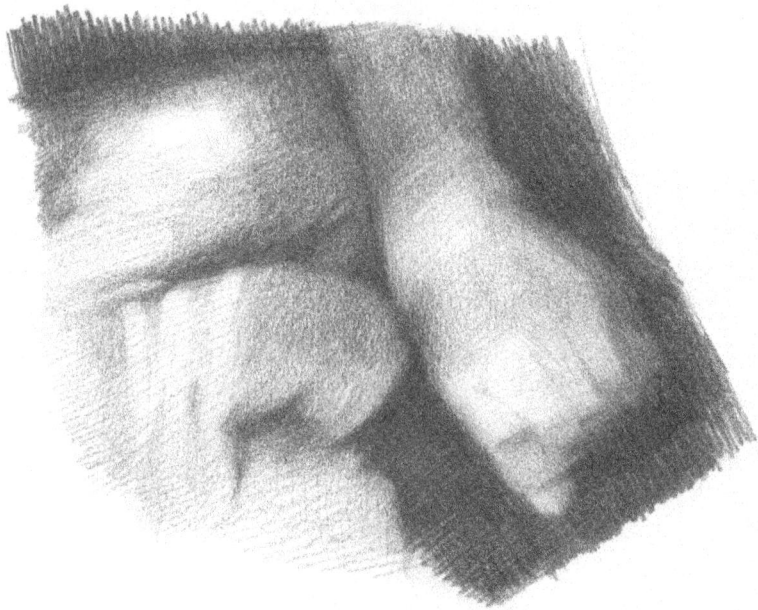

Now go train jiu-jitsu …
(Kid Peligro)

… in an attempt to catch a glimpse … for, is there
anything else one can do? But, it is not as if one ever knows
what one is supposed to catch a glimpse of. For, if the great
stars or seductresses only dazzle because of their absence,[22]
one is always already looking for nothing. But this is not a
nothing in a nihilistic sense of a lack, a missing thing: this
is a nothing in the precise sense of *there is no thing to see, to
find.*

And this is the profound insight in Kid Peligro's signature line. Jiu-jitsu is a craft—thus, one can only experience, or potentially experience, jiu-jitsu through *praxis*. But more importantly it can only be felt "now." Not in a mystical, New Age, sense of 'being aware of oneself in the present' or any such mumbo-jumbo. But in the acknowledgement that there is no "now": that "now" can never be known. For, the moment "now" it uttered, it is already past; or only anticipated. *Now* is a future-anterior moment. Thus, "now" is a metaphor, and more precisely, a catachrestic metaphor—a name. Naming nothing but the openness to the possibility of time.

The "now" always already remains unknown, remaining unknowable—invisible; a remainder.

And it is only in that invisibility, in that wandering—stumbling even—that we might begin to grasp, feel, touch, sense, the invisibility that is jiu-jitsu.

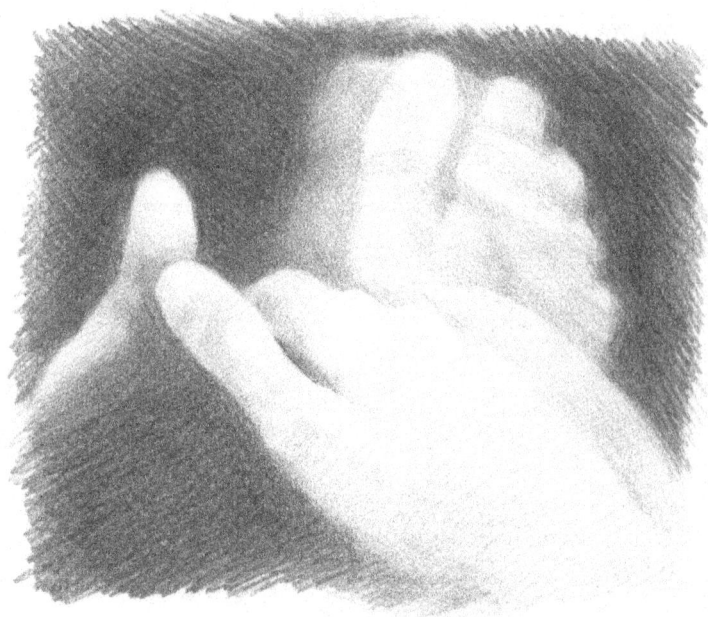

VERMELHA E PRETA

1   Marcelo Dunlop. 'From the treasure chest: Rilion's angle on the guard' in *Graciemag* (5 Sept, 2010): http://www.graciemag.com/en/2010/09/9686/

2   Robert Goodman (Dir). *Rickson Gracie: Choke.* Los Angeles: Propaganda Films, 1999.

3   Slavoj Žižek. *Violence: Six Sideway Reflections.* London: Profile Books, 2008, 122.

4   Immanuel Kant. *Political Writings.* translated by H.B. Nisbet. Cambridge: Cambridge University Press, 1991, 182.

5   The notion of citizen-slave in relation to Spartacus was brought to my attention during a lunch conversation with Alain Badiou at the European Graduate School in Saas Fee, Switzerland, in August 2004.

6   In a conversation with Sean Smith—to whom I remain grateful for kindly, intelligently, and generously helping me develop this piece—he drew my attention to differences between an event and a fight. An event is utterly unknowable till it happens. One can see patterns in fights before they happen (otherwise training for a fight would be utterly futile); thus, they are only relatively unknowable.

However, the fact that fights can change in an instant suggests the presence of unpredictability. So, even as one may have trained well for it, and prepared for 'all eventualities' one can only know if this is so retrospectively: after all, one usually gets beaten not by the technique one did not know (even though this may sometimes be true) but by the move one did not see. Hence, the possibility of blindness accompanies all fights. Thus, even as they may not strictly speaking be events in a philosophical sense, fights and events are close enough for their relationality to be fruitful. Perhaps, the differences between them should not be seen as a source of hindrance but as a possibility for opening new lines of thinking in each other.

7   Advertisement from the Gracie Academy Torrance, *Martial Arts Legends: Special Issue—Gracie Jiu-Jitsu.* (February 1997): 1

8   *ibid*, 1.

9   *ibid*, 1.

10   Todd Hester. 'Saulo Ribeiro: Jiu-Jitsu's Man of Steel' *in Martial Arts Presents: Grappling.* (May 2000): 8.

11   Gilles Deleuze & Félix Guattari. *Kafka: Toward a Minor Literature.* translated by Dana Polan. Minneapolis: University of Minnesota Press, 1986, 19.

12   *ibid,* 19.

13   *ibid,*16.

14   This is in no way a discounting of Luis França's and, later on, Oswaldo Fadda's contributions to jiu-jitsu. Both of them were great practitioners in their own right, with their own contributions to the craft. The fact that Fadda's school bested the Gracie Academy in 1951—wrecking havoc by integrating knowledge of foot locks into the system—would suggest so. Fadda's remixing of jiu-jitsu made such an impression that the Gracies derogatorily termed it *tecnica de suburbano* (suburban techniques): name-calling being surely the highest sign of begrudging respect.

15   Whenever there is scratching, one can also hear echoes of writing. After all, one should not forget that the root of writing is *scratching, tearing: scribere* (Latin), *grapho* (Greek).

Thus, even as it might be tempting to conceive of judo and jiu-jitsu as fixed systems—one where there is a right, and by extension wrong, way to do things—perhaps out of loyalty, love even, to the Gracie Brothers and Kano, one should resist. For, even as they attempted to solve the question of efficiency through leverage, their answers always resounded with further questions. They were always searching, exploring, seeking out. So, even as they found solutions to specific questions, and by doing so re-wrote both judo and jiu-jitsu, each solution was a remix—a scratching. A remixing of the entire system, but one where there is no devastation, annihilation. For, even as each scratching is a tearing, pulling, breaking away, there is always also potentially a creation.

16   Jacques Rancière. *The Aesthetic Unconscious*. translated by Deborah Keates & James Swenson. London: Polity Press, 2009, 4.

17   *ibid*, 6.

18   *ibid*, 6. *italics* from source.

19   *ibid*, 6.

20   *ibid*, 24.

21   *ibid*, 24.

22   Jean Baudrillard. *Seduction.* translated by Brian Singer. New York: St. Martin's Press, 1990, 96.

Jeremy Fernando is the Jean Baudrillard Fellow at the European Graduate School, where he is also a Reader in Contemporary Literature & Thought. He works in the intersections of literature, philosophy, and the media; and has written six books—including *Reading Blindly*, and *Writing Death*. Exploring other media has led him to film, music, and art; and his work has been exhibited in Seoul, Vienna, Hong Kong, and Singapore. He is the editor of the thematic magazine *One Imperative*; and a Fellow of Tembusu College at the National University of Singapore. Even though he has a black belt in judo, he regularly finds himself looking at the ceiling; and he has refined tapping-out into an art, complete with rhythm and form.

Yanyun Chen is an atelier student at the Florence Academy of Art, and a graduate student in philosophy at the European Graduate School. She obtained a BFA (first class) in animation from Nanyang Technological University, and has attended The Animation Workshop in Denmark and Puppetry in Prague programmes. Her works sprout from the melding of drawing, reading, and thinking. She is a nomadic gun-for-hire, and works under the artist names *Piplatchka*, and *Stick and Balloon*— and her crafts traverse animation, illustration, book design, miniature set building, design, and fine art.

The illustrations in this book were referenced from still and moving images of a sparring session between Jeremy Fernando and Terald Hiroyuki Ichige, recorded by Bangles Ong.

www.ingramcontent.com/pod-product-compliance
Lightning Source LLC
Chambersburg PA
CBHW022041090426
42741CB00007B/1153